Reports In American Newspapers -I

by

Swami Vivekananda

Double 9 BOOKS

Reports In American Newspapers -I

by Swami Vivekananda

ISBN: 978-93-59393-51-3

Published by

DOUBLE 9 BOOKS
2/13-B, Ansari Road
Daryaganj, New Delhi – 110002
info@double9books.com
www.double9books.com
Tel. 011-40042856

ABOUT THE AUTHOR

Swami Vivekananda was born Narendranath Datta in India on January 12, 1863. He died on July 4, 1902, and was the most important student of the Indian saint Ramakrishna. He was an important part of bringing Vedanta and Yoga to the West. He is also charged with making people more aware of other religions and making Hinduism a major world religion. Vivekananda had a lot of success at the Parliament. In the years that followed, he gave hundreds of lectures across the United States, England, and Europe to spread the main ideas of Hinduism. He also started the Vedanta Society of New York and the Vedanta Society of San Francisco, which is now the Vedanta Society of Northern California. Both of these groups became the basis for Vedanta Societies in the West. Vivekananda was one of the most important philosophers and social reformers in India at the time. He was also one of the most successful and powerful Vedanta missionaries in the West.People now think of him as one of the most important people in modern India and Hinduism. Mahatma Gandhi said that after reading Vivekananda's works, he loved his country a thousand times more.

CONTENTS

Divinity Of Man

(*Ada Record*, February 28, 1894)

The lecture on the Divinity of Man by Swami Vive Kananda, (In the earlier days Swami Vivekananda's name was thus mis-spelt by the American Press. — Publisher.) the Hindu monk, drew a packed house at the Opera last Friday evening [February 22].

He stated that the fundamental basis of all religions was belief in the soul which is the real man, and something beyond both mind and matter, and proceeded to demonstrate the proposition. The existence of things material are dependent on something else. The mind is mortal because changeable. Death is simply a change.

The soul uses the mind as an instrument and through it affects the body. The soul should be made conscious of its powers. The nature of man is pure and holy but it becomes clouded. In our religion every soul is trying to regain its own nature. The mass of our people believe in the individuality of the soul. We are forbidden to preach that ours is the only true religion. Continuing the speaker said: "I am a spirit and not matter. The religion of the West hopes to again live with their body. Ours teaches there can not be such a state. We say freedom of the soul instead of salvation." The lecture proper lasted but 30 minutes but the president of the lecture committee had announced that at the close of the lecture the speaker would answer any questions propounded him. He gave that opportunity and liberal use was made of the privilege. They came from preachers and professors, physicians and philosophers, from citizens and students, from saints and sinners, some were written but dozens arose in their seats and propounded their questions directly. The speaker responded to all — mark the word, please — in an affable manner and in several instances turned the laugh on the inquirer. They kept up the fusilade for nearly an hour; when the speaker begged to be excused from further labor there yet remained a large pile of unanswered questions. He was an artful dodger on many of the questions. From his answers we glean the following additional statements in regard to the Hindu belief and teachings: They believe in the incarnation of man. One of their teachings is to the effect that their God Krishna was born of a virgin about 5000 years ago in the North of India. The story is very similar to the

Biblical history of Christ, only their God was accidently killed. They believe in evolution and the transmigration of souls: i.e. our souls once inhabited some other living thing, a bird, fish or animal, and on our death will go into some other organism. In reply to the inquiry where these souls were before they came into this world he said they were in other worlds. The soul is the permanent basis of all existence. There was no time when there was no God, therefore no time when there was no creation. Buddhists [sic] do not believe in a personal god; I am no Buddhist. Mohammed is not worshipped in the same sense as Christ. Mohammed believes in Christ but denies he is God. The earth was peopled by evolution and not special selection [creation]. God is the creator and nature the created. We do not have prayer save for the children and then only to improve the mind. Punishment for sin is comparatively immediate. Our actions are not of the soul and can therefore be impure. It is our spirit that becomes perfect and holy. There is no resting place for the soul. It has no material qualities. Man assumes the perfect state when he realizes he is a spirit. Religion is the manifestation of the soul nature. The deeper they see is what makes one holier than another. Worship is feeling the holiness of God. Our religion does not believe in missions and teaches that man should love God for love's sake and his neighbor in spite of himself. The people of the West struggle too hard; repose is a factor of civilization. We do not lay our infirmities to God. There is a tendency toward a union of religions.

Swami Vivekananda On India

(*Bay City Daily Tribune*, March 21, 1894)

Bay City had a distinguished visitor yesterday in the person of Swami Vive Kananda, the much talked of Hindoo monk. He arrived at noon from Detroit where he has been the guest of Senator Palmer and proceeded immediately to the Fraser house. There he was seen by a reporter for *The Tribune*.

Kananda spoke entertainingly of his country and his impressions of this country. He came to America via the Pacific and will return via the Atlantic. "This is a great land," he said, "but I wouldn't like to live here. Americans think too much of money. They give it preference over everything else. Your people have much to learn. When your nation is as old as ours you will be wiser. I like Chicago very much and Detroit is a nice place."

Asked how long he intended remaining in America, he replied: "I do not know. I am trying to see most of your country. I go east next and will spend some time at Boston and New York. I have visited Boston but not to stay. When I have seen America I shall go to Europe. I am very anxious to visit Europe. I have never been there."

Concerning himself the easterner said he was 30 years old. He was born at Calcutta and educated at a college in that city. His profession calls him to all parts of the country, and he is at all times the guest of the nation.

India has a population of 285,000,000," he said. "Of these about 65,000,000 are Mohammedans and most of the others Hindoos. There are only about 600,000 Christians in the country, and of these at least 250,000 are Catholics. Our people do not, as a rule, embrace Christianity; they are satisfied with their own religion. Some go into Christianity for mercenary motives. They are free to do as they wish. We say let everybody have his own faith. We are a cunning nation. We do not believe in bloodshed. There are wicked men in our country and they are in the majority, same as in your country. It is unreasonable to expect people to be angels."

Vive Kananda will lecture in Saginaw to-night

LECTURE LAST NIGHT

The lower floor of the opera house was comfortably filled when the lecture began last evening. Promptly at 8:15 o'clock Swami Vive Kananda made his appearance on the stage, dressed in his beautiful oriental costume. He was introduced in a few words by Dr. C. T. Newkirk.

The first part of the discourse consisted of an explanation of the different religions of India and of the theory of transmigration of souls. In connection with the latter, the speaker said it was on the same basis as the theory of conservation was to the scientist. This latter theory, he said, was first produced by a philosopher of his country. They did not believe in a creation. A creation implied making something out of nothing. That was impossible. There was no beginning of creation, just as there was no beginning of time. God and creation are as two lines — without end, without beginning, without [?] parallel. Their theory of creation is, "It is, was, and is to be." They think all punishment is but re-action. If we put our hand in the fire it is burned. That is the re-action of the action. The future condition of life is determined by the present condition. They do not believe God punishes. "You, in this land," said the speaker, "praise the man who does not get angry and denounce the man who does become angry. And yet thousands of people throughout this country are every day accusing God of being angry. Everybody denounces Nero, who sat and played on his instrument while Rome was burning, and yet thousands of your people are accusing God of doing the same thing today."

The Hindoos have no theory of redemption in their religion. Christ is only to show the way. Every man and woman is a divine being, but covered as though by a screen, which their religion is trying to remove. The removal of that Christians call salvation, they, freedom. God is the creator, preserver, and destroyer of the universe.

The speaker then sought to vindicate the religions of his country. He said it had been proven that the entire system of the Roman Catholic Church had been taken from the books of Buddhism. The people of the west should learn one thing from India — toleration.

Among other subjects which he held up and overhauled were: The Christian missionaries, the zeal of the Presbyterian church and its non-toleration, the dollar-worshipping in this country, and the priests. The latter he said were in the business for the dollars there were in it, and wanted to know how long they would stay in the church if they had to depend on getting their pay from God. After speaking briefly on the Caste system in India, our civilization in the south, our general knowledge of the mind, and various other topics the speaker concluded his remarks.

Religious Harmony

(Saginaw Evening News, March 22, 1894)

Swami Vive Kananda, the much talked of Hindoo monk, spoke to a small but deeply interested audience last evening at the academy of music on "The Harmony of Religions". He was dressed in oriental costume and received an extremely cordial reception. Hon. Rowland Connor gracefully introduced the speaker, who devoted the first portion of his lecture to an explanation of the different religions of India and of the theory of transmigration of souls. The first invaders of India, the Aryans, did not try to exterminate the population of India as the Christians have done when they went into a new land, but the endeavour was made to elevate persons of brutish habits. The Hindoo is disgusted with those people of his own country who do not bathe and who eat dead animals. The Northern people of India have not tried to force their customs on the southerns, but the latter gradually adopted many ways of the former class. In southernmost portions of India there are a few persons who are Christians and who have been so for thousands [?] of years. The Spaniards came to Ceylon with Christianity. The Spaniards thought that their God commanded them to kill and murder and to tear down heathen temples.

If there were not different religions no one religion would survive. The Christian needs his selfish religion. The Hindoo needs his own creed. Those which were founded on a book still stand. Why could not the Christian convert the Jew? Why could they not make the Persians Christians? Why not so with the Mohammedans? Why cannot any impression be made upon China or Japan? The Buddhists, the first missionary religion, have double the number of converts of any other religion and they did not use the sword. The Mohammedans used the most force, and they number the least of the three great missionary, religions. The Mohammedans have had their day. Every day you read of Christian nations acquiring land by bloodshed. What missionaries preach against this? Why should the most bloodthirsty nations exalt an alleged religion which is not the religion of Christ? The Jews and the Arabs were the fathers of Christianity, and how have they been persecuted by the Christians! The Christians have been weighed in the balance in India and found wanting.

The speaker did not wish to be unkind, but he wanted to show Christians how they looked in other eyes. The Missionaries who preach the burning pit are regarded with horror. The Mohammedans rolled wave after wave over India, waving the sword, and today where are they? The farthest that all religions can see is the existence of a spiritual entity. So no religion can teach beyond this point. In every religion there is the essential truth and nonessential casket in which this jewel lies. The believing in the Jewish book or the Hindoo book is non-essential. Circumstances change, the receptacle is different; but the central truth remains. The essentials being the same, the educated people of every community retain the essentials. The shell of the oyster is not attractive, but the pearls are within. Before a small fraction of the world is converted Christianity will be divided into many creeds. That is the law of nature. Why take a single instrument from the great religious orchestras of the earth? Let the grand symphony go on. Be pure, urged the speaker, give up superstition and see the wonderful harmony of nature. Superstition gets the better of religion. All the religions are good since the essentials are the same. Each man should have the perfect exercise of his individuality but these individualities form a perfect whole. This marvellous condition is already in existence. Each creed has had something to add to the wonderful structure.

The speaker sought throughout to vindicate the religions of his country and said that it had been proven that the entire system of the Roman Catholic Church had been taken from the books of Buddhism. He dilated at some length on the high code of morality and purity of life that the ethics of Buddha taught but allowed that as far as the belief in the personality of God was concerned, agnosticism prevailed, the main thing being to follow out Buddha's precepts which were, "Be good, be moral, be perfect."

From Far Off India

(Saginaw Courier-Herald, March 22, 1894)

Seated in the lobby of the Hotel Vincent yesterday evening was a strong and regular featured man of fine presence, whose swarthy skin made more pronounced the pearly whiteness of his even teeth. Under a broad and high forehead his eyes betoken intelligence. This gentleman was Swami Vive Kananda, the Hindoo preacher. Mr. Kananda's conversation is in pure and grammatically constructed English sentences, to which his slightly foreign accent lends piquancy. Readers of the Detroit papers are aware that Mr. Kananda has lectured in that city a number of times and aroused the animosity of some on account of his strictures upon Christians. *The Courier-Herald* representative had a few moments' conversation with the learned Buddhist [?] just before he left for the Academy, where he was to lecture. Mr. Kananda said in conversation that he was surprised at the lapses from the paths of rectitude which were so common among Christians, but that there was good and bad to be found among members of all religious bodies. One statement he made was decidedly un-American. Upon being asked if he had been investigating our institutions, he replied: "No, I am a preacher only." This displayed both a want of curiosity and narrowness, which seemed foreign to one who appeared to be so well versed upon religious topics as did the Buddhist [?] preacher.

From the hotel to the Academy was but a step and at 8 o'clock Rowland Connor introduced to a small audience the lecturer, who was dressed in a long orange colored robe, fastened by a red sash, and who wore a turban of windings of what appeared to be a narrow shawl.

The lecturer stated at the opening that he had not come as a missionary, and that it was not the part of a Buddhist to convert others from their faiths and beliefs. He said that the subject of his address would be, "The Harmony of Religions". Mr. Kananda said that many ancient religions had been founded, and were dead and gone.

He said that the Buddhists [Hindus] comprise two-thirds of the race, and that the other third comprised those of all other believers. He said that the Buddhists have no place of future torment for men. In that they differ from the Christians, who will forgive a man for five minutes in this world and condemn him to everlasting punishment in the next. Buddha was the first to teach the universal brotherhood of man. It is a cardinal principle of the Buddhist faith today. The Christian preaches it, but does not practice its own teachings.

He instanced the condition of the Negro in the South, who is not allowed in hotels nor to ride in the same cars with white men, and is a being to whom no decent man will speak. He said that he had been in the South, and spoke from his knowledge and observation.

An Evening With Our Hindu Cousins

(Northampton Daily Herald, April 16, 1894)

For Swami Vive Kananda proved conclusively that all our neighbors across the water, even the remotest, are our close cousins differing only a trifle in color, language, customs and religion, the silver-tongued Hindu monk prefacing his address in city hall Saturday evening [April 14] by an historic sketch of the origin of his own and all other leading nations of the earth which demonstrated the truth that race-kinship is more of a simple fact than many know or always care to admit.

The informal address that followed regarding some of the customs of the Hindu people was more of the nature of a pleasant parlor talk, expressed with the easy freedom of the conversational adept, and to those of his hearers possessing a natural and cultivated interest in the subject both the man and his thought were intensely interesting for more reasons than can be given here. But to others the speaker was disappointing in not covering a larger scope in his word-pictures, the address, although extremely lengthy for the American lecture-platform, referring to very few of the "customs and manners" of the peculiar people considered, and of whose personal, civil, home, social and religious life much more would have been gladly heard from this one of the finest representatives of this oldest of races, which the average student of human nature should find preeminently interesting but really knows the least about.

The allusions to the life of the Hindu began with a picture of the birth of the Hindu boy, his introduction to educational training, his marriage, slight reference to the home life but not what was expected, the speaker diverging frequently to make comparative comments on the customs and ideas of his own and English-speaking races, socially, morally and religiously, the inference in all cases being clearly in favor of his own, although most courteously, kindly and gracefully expressed. Some of his auditors who are tolerably well posted as to social and family conditions among the Hindoos of all classes would have liked to have asked the speaker a challenging question or two on a good many of the points he touched upon. For instance, when he so eloquently and beautifully portrayed the Hindu idea of womanhood as the divine motherhood ideal, to be forever reverenced, even worshipped with a devotion of loyalty such as the most woman-respecting unselfish and truest of American sons, husbands and fathers cannot even conceive of, one would have liked to know what the reply would have been to the query as to how far this beautiful theory is exemplified in practice in the majority of Hindu homes. which hold wives, mothers, daughters and sisters.

The rebuke to the greed for gain, the national vice of luxury-seeking, self-seeking the "dollar-caste" sentiment which taints the dominant white European and American races to their mortal danger, morally and civilly, was only too just and superbly well-put, the slow, soft, quiets unimpassioned musical voice embodying its thought with all the power and fire of the most vehement physical utterance, and went straight to the mark like the "Thou art the man" of the prophet. But when this learned Hindu nobleman by birth, nature and culture attempts to prove — as he repeatedly did in his frequent and apparently half-unconscious digressions from the special point under consideration — that the distinctively self-centred, self-cultivating, preeminently self-soulsaving, negative and passive, not to say selfishly indolent religion of his race has proven itself superior in its usefulness to the world to the vitally aggressive, self-forgetful, do-good unto-others-first-last-and-always, go-ye-into-all-the-world and *work* religion which we call Christianity, in whose name nine tenths of all the really practical moral, spiritual and philanthropic work of the world has been and is being done, whatever sad and gross mistakes have been made by its unwise zealots, he attempts a large contract.

But to see and hear Swami Vive Kananda is an opportunity which no intelligent fair-minded American ought to miss if one cares to see a shining light of the very finest product of the mental, moral and spiritual culture of a race which reckons its age by thousands where we count ours by hundreds and is richly worth the study of every mind.

Sunday afternoon [April 15] the distinguished Hindu spoke to the students of Smith college at the vesper service, the Fatherhood of God and the Brotherhood of man being, virtually, his theme, and that the address made a deep impression is evinced by the report of every auditor, the broadest liberality of true religious sentiment and precept characterizing the whole trend of thought.

The Manners And Customs Of India

(*Boston Herald*, May 15, 1894)

Association Hall was crowded with ladies yesterday, to hear Swami Vivekananda, the Brahmin (Meaning Hindu. – Publisher.) Monk talk about "The Religion of India" [actually "The Manners and Customs of India"], for the benefit of the ward 16 day nursery [actually, Tyler-street Day Nursery]. The Brahmin monk has become a fad in Boston, as he was in Chicago last year, and his earnest, honest, cultured manner has won many friends for him.

The Hindoo nation is not given to marriage, he said, not because we are women haters, but because our religion teaches us to worship women. The Hindoo is taught to see in every woman his mother, and no man wants to marry his mother. God is mother to us. We don't care anything about God in heaven; it is mother to us. We consider marriage a low vulgar state, and if a man does marry, it is because he needs a helpmate for religion.

You say we ill-treat our women. What nation in the world has not ill-treated its women? In Europe or America a man can marry a woman for money, and, after capturing her dollars, can kick her out. In India, on the contrary, when a woman marries for money, her children are considered slaves, according to our teaching, and when a rich man marries, his money passes into the hands of his wife, so that he would be scarcely likely to turn the keeper of his money out of doors.

You say we are heathens, we are uneducated, uncultivated, but we laugh in our sleeves at your want of refinement in telling us such things. With us, quality and birth make caste, not money. No amount of money can do anything for you in India. In caste the poorest is as good as the richest, and that is one of the most beautiful things about it.

Money has made warfare in the world, and caused Christians to trample on each other's necks. Jealousy, hatred and avariciousness are born of money-getters. Here it is all work, hustle and bustle. Caste saves a man from all this. It makes it possible for a man to live with less money, and it brings work to all. The man of caste has time to think of his soul; and that is what we want in the society of India.

The Brahmin is born to worship God, and the higher his caste, the greater his social restrictions are. Caste has kept us alive as a nation, and while it has many defects, it has many more advantages.

Mr. Vivekananda described the universities and colleges of India, both ancient and modern, notably the one at Benares, that has 20,000 students and professors.

When you judge my religion, he continued, you take it that yours is perfect and mine wrong; and when you criticise the society of India you suppose it to be uncultured just so far as it does not conform to your standard. That is nonsense.

In reference to the matter of education, the speaker said that the educated men of India become professors, while the less educated become priests.

The Religions Of India

(*Boston Herald*, May 17, 1894)

The Brahmin monk, Swami Vivekananda, lectured yesterday afternoon in Association Hall on "The Religions of India", in aid of the Ward 16 Day Nursery. There was a large attendance.

The speaker first gave an account of the Mahommedans, who formed, he said, one-fifth of the population. They believed in both Old and New Testaments, but Jesus Christ they regarded only as a prophet. They had no church organization, though there was reading of the Koran.

The Parsees, another race, called their sacred book the Zend-Avesta, and believed in two warring deities, Armuzd the good and Ahriman the evil. They believed that finally the good would triumph over the evil. Their moral code was summed up in the words: "Good thought, good words, good deeds."

The Hindus proper looked up to the Vedas as their religious scripture. They held each individual to the customs of caste, but gave him full liberty to think for himself in religious matters. A part of their method was to seek out some holy man or prophet in order to take advantage of the spiritual current that flowed through him.

The Hindus had three different schools of religion — the dualistic, the qualified monistic and the monistic — and these three were regarded as stages through which each individual naturally passed in the course of his religious development.

All three believed in God, but the dualistic school believed that God and man were separate entities, while the monistic declared that there was only one existence in the universe, this unitary existence teeing neither God nor soul, but something beyond.

The lecturer quoted from the Vedas to show the character of the Hindu religion, and declared that, to find God, one must search one's own heart.

Religion did not consist of pamphlets or books; it consisted of looking into the human heart, and finding there the truths of God and immortality.

"Whomsoever I like," said the Vedas, "him I create a prophet," and to be a prophet was all there was of religion.

The speaker brought his lecture to a close by giving an account of the Jains, who show remarkable kindness to dumb animals, and whose moral law is summed up in the words: "Not to injure others is the highest good."

Sects And Doctrines In India

(*Harvard Crimson*, May 17, 1894)

Swami Vivekananda, the Hindoo monk, gave an address last evening in Sever Hall under the auspices of the Harvard Religious Union. The address was very interesting, the clear and eloquent voice of the speaker, and his low, earnest delivery making his words singularly impressive.

There are various sects and doctrines in India, said Vivekananda, some of which accept the theory of a personal God, and others which believe that God and the universe are one; but whatever sect the Hindoo belongs to he does not say that his is the only right belief, and that all others must be wrong. He believes that there are many ways of coming to God; that a man who is truly religious rises above the petty quarrels of sects or creed. In India if a man believes that he is a spirit, a soul, and not a body, then he is said to have religion and not till then.

To become a monk in India it is necessary to lose all thought of the body; to look upon other human beings as souls. So monks can never marry. Two vows are taken when a man becomes a monk, poverty and chastity. He is not allowed to receive or possess any money whatever. The first ceremony to be performed on joining the order is to be burnt in effigy, which supposed to destroy once for all the old body, name and caste. The man then receives a new name, and is allowed to go forth and preach or travel, but must take no money for what he does.

Less Doctrine And More Bread

(*Baltimore American*, October 15, 1894)

The Lyceum Theater was crowded last night at the first of a series of meetings by the Vrooman Brothers. The subject discussed was "Dynamic Religion".

Swami Vivekananda, the high priest [?] from India, was the last speaker. He spoke briefly, and was listened to with marked attention. His English and his mode of delivery were excellent. There is a foreign accent to his syllables, but not enough to prevent him from being plainly understood. He was dressed in the costume of his native country, which was decidedly picturesque. He said he could speak but briefly after the oratory that had preceded him, but he could add his endorsement to all that had been said. He had traveled a great deal, and preached to all kinds of people. He had found that the particular kind of doctrine preached made little difference. What is wanted is practical sort of work. If such ideas could not be carried out, he would lose his faith in humanity. The cry all over the world is "less doctrine and more bread". He thought the sending of missionaries to India all right; he had no objections to offer, but he thought it would be better to send fewer men and more money. So far as India was concerned, she had religious doctrine to spare. Living up to the doctrines was needed more than more doctrines. The people of India, as well as the people all over the world, had been taught to pray, but prayer with the lips was not enough; people should pray with their hearts. "A few people in the world," he said, "really try to do good. Others look on and applaud, and think that they themselves have done great good. Life is love, and when a man ceases to do good to others, he is dead spiritually."

On Sunday evening next Swami Vivekananda will make the address of the evening at the Lyceum.

(*Sun*, October 15, 1894)

Vivekananda sat on the stage last night with imperturbable stolidity until it came his turn to speak. Then his manner changed and he spoke with force and feeling. He followed the Vrooman brothers and said there was little to add to what had been said save his testimony as a "man from the Antipodes".

"We have doctrines enough," he continued. "What we want now is practical work as presented in these speeches. When asked about the missionaries sent to India I reply all right. But we want money more and men less. India has bushels full of doctrines and to spare. What is wanted is the means to carry them out.

"Prayer may be done in different ways. Prayer with the hands is yet higher than prayer with the lips and is more saving.

"All religions teach us to do good for our brothers. Doing good is nothing extraordinary — it is the only way to live. Everything in nature tends to expansion for life and contraction for death. It is the same in religion. Do good by helping others without ulterior motives. The moment this ceases contraction and death follow."

The Religion Of Buddha

(*Morning Herald*, October 22, 1894)

An audience which filled the Lyceum Theatre [Baltimore] from pit to dome assembled last night at the second of the series of meetings held by the Vrooman Brothers in the interest of "Dynamic Religion". Fully 3,000 persons were present. Addresses were made by the Rev. Hiram Vrooman, Rev. Walter Vrooman and Rev. Swarri Vivekananda, the Brahmin High Priest now visiting this city. The speakers of the evening were seated on the stage, the Rev. Vivekananda being an object of particular interest to all. He wore a yellow turban and a red robe tied in at the waste [sic] with a sash of the same color, which added to the Oriental cast of his features and invested him with a peculiar interest. His personality seemed to be the feature of the evening. His address was delivered in an easy, unembarrassed manner, his diction being perfect and his accent similar to that of a cultured member of the Latin race familiar with the English language. He said in part:

THE HIGH PRIEST SPEAKS

"Buddha began to found the religion of India 600 years before the birth of Christ He found the religion of India at that time mainly engaged in eternal discussions upon the nature of the human soul. There was no remedy according to the ideas then prevailing for the cure of religious ills but sacrifices of animals, sacrificial altars and similar methods.

"In the midst of this system a priest [?] was born who was a member of one of the leading families who was the founder of Buddhism. His was, in the first place, not the founding of a new religion, but a movement of reformation. He believed in the good of all. His religion, as formulated by him, consisted of the discovery of three things: First, 'There is an evil'; second, 'What is the cause of this evil?' This he ascribed to the desires of men to be superior to others, an evil that could be cured by unselfishness. Third, 'This evil is curable by becoming unselfish'. Force, he concluded, could not cure it; dirt cannot wash dirt; hate cannot cure hate.

"This was the basis of his religion. So long as society tries to cure human selfishness by laws and institutions whose aim is to force others to do good to their neighbors, nothing can be done. The remedy is not to place trick against trick and force against force. The only remedy is in making unselfish men and women. You may enact laws to cure present evils, but they will be of no avail.

"Buddha found in India too much talking about God and His essence and too little work. He always insisted upon this fundamental truth, that we are to be pure and holy, and that we are to help others to be holy also. He believed that man must go to work and help others; find his soul in others; find his life in others. He believed that in the conjunction of doing good to others is the only good we do ourselves. [sic] He believed that there was always in the world too much theory and too little practice. A dozen Buddhas in India at the present time would do good, and one Buddha in this country would also be beneficial.

"When there is too much doctrine, too much belief in my father's religion, too much rational superstition, a change is needed. Such doctrine produces evil, and a reformation is necessary."

At the conclusion of Mr. Vivekananda's address there was a hearty burst of applause.

(*Baltimore American*, October 22, 1894)

The Lyceum Theater was crowded to the doors last night at the second meeting of the series conducted by the Vrooman brothers on "Dynamic Religion". Swami Vivekananda, of India, made the principal address. He spoke on the Buddhist religion, and told of the evils which existed among the people of India, at the time of the birth of Buddha. The social inequalities in India, he said, were at that period a thousand times greater than anywhere else in the world. "Six hundred years before Christ," he continued, "the priesthood of India exercised great influence over the minds of the people, and between the upper and nether millstone of intellectuality and learning the people were ground. Buddhism, which is the religion of more than two-third of the human family, was not founded as an entirely new religion, but rather as a reformation which carried off the corruption of the times. Buddha seems to have been the only prophet who did everything for others and absolutely nothing for himself. He gave up his home and all the enjoyments of life to spend his days in search of the medicine for the terrible disease of human misery. In an age when men and priests were discussing the essence of the deity, he discovered what people had overlooked, that misery existed. The cause of evil is our desire to be superior to others and our selfishness. The moment that the world becomes unselfish all evil will vanish. So long as society tries to cure evil by laws and institutions, evil will not be cured. The world has tried this method ineffectually for thousands of years. Force against force never cures, and the only cure for evil is unselfishness. We need to teach people to obey the laws rather than to make more laws. Buddhism was the first missionary religion of the world but it was one of the teachings of Buddhism not to antagonize any other religion. Sects weaken their power for good by making war on each other."

All Religions Are Good

(*Washington Post*, October 29, 1894)

Mr. Kananda spoke yesterday at the People's Church on the invitation of Dr. Kent, pastor of the church. His talk in the morning was a regular sermon, dealing entirely with the spiritual side of religion, and presenting the, to orthodox sects, rather original proposition that there is good in the foundation of every religion, that all religions, like languages, are descended from a common stock, and that each is good in its corporal and spiritual aspects so long as it is kept free from dogma and fossilism. The address in the afternoon was more in the form of a lecture on the Aryan race, and traced the descent of the various allied nationalities by their language, religion and customs from the common Sanskrit stock.

After the meeting, to a *Post* reporter Mr. Kananda said: "I claim no affiliation with any religious sect, but occupy the position of an observer, and so far as I may, of a teacher to mankind. All religion to me is good. About the higher mysteries of life and existence I can do no more than speculate, as others do. Reincarnation seems to me to be the nearest to a logical explanation for many things with which we are confronted in the realm of religion. But I do not advance it as a doctrine. It is no more than a theory at best, and is not susceptible of proof except by personal experience, and that proof is good only for the man who has it. Your experience is nothing to me, nor mine to you. I am not a believer in miracles — they are repugnant to me in matters of religion. You might bring the world tumbling down about my ears, but that would be no proof to me that there was a God, or that you worked by his agency, if there was one.

HE BELIEVES IT BLINDLY

"I must, however, believe in a past and a hereafter as necessary to the existence of the present. And if we go on from here, we must go in other forms, and so comes any belief in reincarnation. But I can prove nothing, and any one is welcome to deprive me of the theory of reincarnation provided they will show me something better to replace it. Only up to the present I have found nothing that offers so satisfactory an explanation to me."

Mr. Kananda is a native of Calcutta, and a graduate of the government university there. He speaks English like a native, having received his university training in that tongue. He has had good opportunity to observe the contact between the native and the English, and it would disappoint a foreign missionary worker to hear him speak in very unconcerned style of the attempts to convert the natives. In this connection he was asked what effect the Western teaching was having on the thought of the Orient.

"Of course," he said, "no thought of any sort can come into a country without having its effect, but the effect of Christian teaching on Oriental thought is, if it exists, so small as to be imperceptible. The Western doctrines have made about as much impression there as have the Eastern doctrines here, perhaps not so much. That is, among the higher thinkers of the country. The effect of the missionary work among the masses is imperceptible. When converts are made they of course drop at once out of the native sects, but the mass of the population is so great that the converts of the missionaries have very little effect that can be seen."

THE YOGIS ARE JUGGLERS

When asked whether he knew anything of the alleged miraculous performances of the yogis and adepts Mr. Kananda replied that he was not interested in miracles, and that while there were of course a great many clever jugglers in the country, their performances were tricks. Mr. Kananda said that he had seen the mango trick but once, and then by a fakir on a small scale. He held the same view about the alleged attainments of the lamas. "There is a great lack of trained, scientific, and unprejudiced observers in all accounts of these phenomena," said he, "so that it is hard to select the false from the true."

The Hindu View Of Life

(*Brooklyn Times*, December 31, 1894)

The Brooklyn Ethical Association, at the Pouch Gallery last night, tendered a reception to Swami Vivekananda. . . . Previous to the reception the distinguished visitor delivered a remarkably interesting lecture on "The Religions of India". Among other things he said:

"The Hindoo's view of life is that we are here to learn; the whole happiness of life is to learn; the human soul is here to love learning and get experience. I am able to read my Bible better by your Bible, and you will learn to read your Bible the better by my Bible. If there is but one religion to be true, all the rest must be true. The same truth has manifested itself in different forms, and the forms are according to the different circumstances of the physical or mental nature of the different nations.

"If matter and its transformation answer for all that we have, there is no necessity for supposing the existence of a soul. But it can [not] be proven that thought has been evolved out of matter. We can not deny that bodies inherit certain tendencies, but those tendencies only mean the physical configuration through which a peculiar mind alone can act in a peculiar way. These peculiar tendencies in that soul have been caused by past actions. A soul with a certain tendency will take birth in a body which is the fittest instrument for the display of that tendency, by the laws of affinity. And this is in perfect accord with science, for science wants to explain everything by habit, and habit is got through repetitions. So these repetitions are also necessary to explain the natural habits of a new-born soul. They were not got in this present life; therefore, they must have come down from past lives.

"All religions are so many stages. Each one of them represents the stage through which the human soul passes to realize God. Therefore, not one of them should be neglected. None of the stages are dangerous or bad. They are good. Just as a child becomes a young man, and a young man becomes an old man, so they are travelling from truth to truth; they become dangerous only when they become rigid, and will not move further — when he ceases to grow. If the child refuses to become an old man, then he is diseased, but if they steadily grow, each step will lead them onward until they reach the whole truth. Therefore, we believe in both a personal and impersonal

Ideals Of Womanhood

(Brooklyn Standard Union, January 21, 1895)

Swami Vivekananda, after being presented to the audience by Dr. Janes, president of the Ethical Association, said in part:

"The product of the slums of any nation cannot be the criterion of our judgment of that nation. One may collect the rotten, worm-eaten apples under every apple tree in the world, and write a book about each of them, and still know nothing of the beauty and possibilities of the apple tree. Only in the highest and best can we judge a nation — the fallen are a race by themselves. Thus it is not only proper, but just and right, to judge a custom by its best, by its ideal.

"The ideal of womanhood centres in the Arian race of India, the most ancient in the worlds history. In that race, men and women were priests, 'sabatimini [saha-dharmini],' or co-religionists, as the Vedas call them. There every family had its hearth or altar, on which, at the time of the wedding, the marriage fire was kindled, which was kept alive, until either spouse died, when the funeral pile was lighted from its spark. There man and wife together offered their sacrifices, and this idea was carried so far that a man could not even pray alone, because it was held that he was only half a being, for that reason no unmarried man could become a priest. The same held true in ancient Rome and Greece.

"But with the advent of a distinct and separate priest-class, the co-priesthood of the woman in all these nations steps back. First it was the Assyrian race, coming of semitic blood, which proclaimed the doctrine that girls have no voice, and no right, even when married. The Persians drank deep of this Babylonian idea, and by them it was carried to Rome and to Greece, and everywhere woman degenerated.

"Another cause was instrumental in bringing this about — the change in the system of marriage. The earliest system was a matriarchal one; that is, one in which the mother was the centre, and in which the girls acceded to her station. This led to the curious system of the Polianders [polyandrous], where five and six brothers often married one wife. Even the Vedas contain a trace of it in the provision, that when a man died without leaving any children, his widow was permitted to live with another man, until she became a mother; but the children she bore did not belong to their father, but to her dead husband. In later years the widow was allowed to marry again, which the modern idea forbids her to do.

"But side by side with these excrescences a very intense idea of personal purity sprang up in the nation. On every page the Vedas preach personal purity. The laws in this respect were extremely strict. Every boy and girl was sent to the university, where they studied until their twentieth or thirtieth year; there the least impurity was punished almost cruelly. This idea of personal purity has imprinted itself deeply into the very heart of the race, amounting almost to a mania. The most conspicuous example of it is to be found in the capture of Chito [Chitor] by the Mohammedans. The men defended the town against tremendous odds; and when the women saw that defeat was inevitable they lit a monstrous fire on the market place, and when the enemy broke down the gates 74,500 women jumped on the huge funeral pile and perished in the flames. This noble example has been handed down in India to the present time, when every letter bears the words '74,500,' which means that any one who unlawfully reads the letter, thereby becomes guilty of a crime similar to the one which drove those noble women of Chito to their death.

"The next period is that of the monks; it came with the advent of Buddhism, which taught that only the monks could reach the 'nirvana', something similar to the Christian heaven. The result was that all India became one huge monastery; there was but one object, one battle — to remain pure. All the blame was cast onto women, and even the proverbs warned against them. 'What is the gate to hell?' was one of them, to which the answer was: 'Woman'. Another read: 'What is the chain which binds us all to dust? Woman'. Another one: 'Who is the blindest of the blind? He who is deceived by woman.'

"The same idea is to be found in the cloisters of the West. The development of all monasticism always meant the degeneration of women.

"But eventually another idea of womanhood arose. In the West it found its ideal in the wife, in India in the mother. But do not think that the priests were altogether responsible for this change. I know they always lay claim to everything in the world and I say this, although I am myself a priest. I'll bend my knees to every prophet in every religion and clime, but candor compels me to say, that here in the West the development of women was brought about by men like John Stuart Mill and the revolutionary French philosophers. Religion has done something, no doubt, but not all. Why, in Asia Minor, Christian bishops to this day keep a harem!

"The Christian ideal is that which is found in the Anglo-Saxon race. The Mohammedan woman differs vastly from her western sisters in so far as her social and intellectual development is not so pronounced. But do not, on that account, think that the Mohammedan woman is unhappy, because it is not so. In India woman has enjoyed property rights since thousands of years. Here a man may disinherit his wife, in India the whole estate of the deceased husband must go to the wife, personal property absolutely, real property for life.

"In India the mother is the centre of the family and our highest ideal, She is to us the representative of God, as God is the mother of the Universe. It was a female sage who first found the unity of God, and laid down this doctrine in one of the first hymns of the Vedas. Our God is both personal and absolute, the absolute is male, the personal, female. And thus it comes that we now say: 'The first manifestation of God is the hand that rocks the cradle.' He is of the 'arian' race, who is born through prayer, and he is a nonarian, who is born through sensuality.

"This doctrine of prenatal influence is now slowly being recognized, and science as well as religion calls out: 'Keep yourself holy, and pure.' So deeply has this been recognized in India, that there we even speak of adultery in marriage, except when marriage is consummated in prayer. And I and every good Hindoo believe, that my mother was pure and holy, and hence I owe her everything that I am. That is the secret of the race — chastity."

True Buddhism

(Brooklyn Standard Union, February 4, 1895)

Swami Vivekananda, being presented by Dr. Janes, the president of the Ethical Association, under whose auspices these lectures are given, said in part: "The Hindoo occupies a unique position towards Buddhism. Like Christ, who antagonized the Jews, Buddha antagonized the prevailing religion of India; but while Christ was rejected by his countrymen, Buddha was accepted as God Incarnate. He denounced the priestcraft at the very doors of their temples, yet to-day he is worshipped by them.

"Not, however, the creed which bears his name. What Buddha taught, the Hindoo believes, but what the Buddhists teach, we do not accept. For the teachings of the Great Master, spread out broadcast over the land, came back in tradition, colored by the channels through which they passed.

"In order to understand Buddhism fully we must go-back to the mother religion from which it came. The books of Veda have two parts; the first, Cura makanda [Karma Kanda], contains the sacrificial portion, while the second part, the Vedanta, denounces sacrifices, teaching charity and love, but not death. Each sect took up what portion it liked. The charvaka, or materialist, basing his doctrine on the first part, believed that all was matter and that there is neither a heaven nor a hell, neither a soul nor a God. The second sect, the Gains [Jains], were very moral atheists, who, while rejecting the idea of a God, believed that there is a soul, striving for more perfect development. These two sects were called the heretics. A third sect was called orthodox, because it accepted the Vedas, although it denied the existence of a personal God, believing that everything sprang from the atom or nature.

"Thus the intellectual world was divided before Buddha came. But for a correct understanding of his religion, it is also necessary to speak of the caste then existing. The Vedas teach that he who knows God is a Brahma [Brâhmin]; he who protects his fellows is a Chocta [Kshatriya], while he who gains his livelihood in trade is a Visha [Vaishya]. These different social diversions [divisions] developed or degenerated into iron-bound casts [castes], and an organized and crystallized priestcraft stood upon the neck of the nation. At this time Buddha was born, and his religion is therefore the culmination of an attempt at a religious and a social reformation.

"The air was full of the din of discussion; 20,000 blind priests were trying to lead 20,000,000 [?] blind men, fighting amongst themselves. What was more needed at that time than for a Buddha to preach? 'Stop quarreling, throw your books aside, be perfect!' Buddha never fought true castes, for they are nothing but the congregation of those of a particular natural tendency, and they are always valuable. But Buddha fought the degenerated castes with their hereditary privileges, and spoke to the Brahmins: 'True Brahmins are not greedy, nor criminal nor angry — are you such? If not, do not mimic the genuine, real men. Caste is a state, not an iron-bound class, and every one who knows and loves God is a true Brahmin.' And with regard to the sacrifices, he said: 'Where do the Vedas say that sacrifices make us pure? They may please, perhaps, the angels, but they make us no better. Hence, let off these mummeries — love God and strive to be perfect.'

"In later years these doctrines of Buddha were forgotten. Going to lands yet unprepared for the reception of these noble truths, they came back tainted with the foibles of these nations. Thus the Nihilists arose — a sect whose doctrine it was that the whole universe, God and soul, had no basis, but that everything is continually changing. They believed in nothing but the enjoyment of the moment, which eventually resulted in the most revolting orgies. That, however, is not the doctrine of Buddha, but a horrible degeneration of it, and honor to the Hindoo nation, who stood up and drove it out.

"Every one of Buddha's teachings is founded in the Vedantas. He was one of those monks who wanted to bring out the truths, hidden in those books and in the forest monasteries. I do not believe that the world is ready for them even now; it still wants those lower religions, which teach of a personal God. Because of this, the original Buddhism could not hold the popular mind, until it took up the modifications, which were reflected back from Thibet and the Tartars. Original Buddhism was not at all nihilistic. It was but an attempt to combat cast and priestcraft; it was the first in the world to stand as champion of the dumb animals, the first to break down the caste, standing between man and man."

Swami Vivekananda concluded his lecture with the presentation of a few pictures from the life of Buddha, the "great one, who never thought a thought and never performed a deed except for the good of others; who had the greatest intellect and heart, taking in all mankind and all the animals, all embracing, ready to give up his life for the highest angels as well as for the lowest worm." He first showed how Buddha, for the purpose of saving a herd of sheep, intended for a king's sacrifice, had thrown himself upon the altar, and thus accomplished his purpose. He next pictured how the great prophet had parted from his wife and baby at the cry of suffering mankind, and how, lastly, after his teachings had been universally accepted in India, he accepted the invitation of a despised Pariah, who dined him on swine's flesh, from the effects of which he died.

India's Gift To The World

(Brooklyn Standard Union, February 27, 1895)

Swami Vivekananda, the Hindoo monk, delivered a lecture Monday night under the auspices of the Brooklyn Ethical Association before a fairly large audience at the hall of the Long Island Historical Society, corner Pierrepont and Clinton streets. His subject was "India's Gift to the World".

He spoke of the wondrous beauties of his native land, "where stood the earliest cradle of ethics, arts, sciences, and literature, and the integrity of whose sons and the virtue of whose daughters have been sung by all travelers." Then the lecturer showed in rapid details, what India has given to the world.

"In religion," he said, "she has exerted a great influence on Christianity, as the very teachings of Christ would [could] be traced back to those of Buddha." He showed by quotations from the works of European and American scientists the many points of similarity between Buddha and Christ. The latter's birth, his seclusion from the world, the number of his apostles, and the very ethics of his teachings are the same as those of Buddha, living many hundred years before him.

"Is it mere chance," the lecturer asked, "or was Buddha's religion but the foreshadowing of that of Christ? The majority of your thinkers seem to be satisfied in the latter explanation, but there are some bold enough to say that Christianity is the direct offspring of Buddhism just as the earliest heresy in the Christian religion — the Monecian [Manichaean] heresy — is now universally regarded as the teaching of a sect of Buddhists. But there is more evidence that Christianity is founded in Buddhism. We find it in recently discovered inscriptions from the reign of Emperor Oshoka [Asoka] of India, about 300 B.C., who made treaties with all the Grecian kings, and whose missionaries discriminated [disseminated ?] in those very parts, where, centuries after, Christianity flourished, the principles of the Buddhistic religion. Thus it is explained, why you have our doctrine of trinity, of incarnation of God, and of our ethics, and why the service in our temples is so much alike to that in your present Catholic churches, from the mass to the chant and benediction. Buddhism had all these long before you. Now use your own judgment on these premise — we Hindoos stand ready to be convinced that yours is the earlier religion, although we had ours some three hundred years before yours was even thought of.

"The same holds good with respect to sciences. India has given to antiquity the earliest scientifical physicians, and, according to Sir William Hunter, she has even contributed to modern medical science by the discovery of various chemicals and by teaching you how to reform misshapen ears and noses. Even more it has done in mathematics, for algebra, geometry, astronomy, and the triumph of modern science — mixed mathematics — were all invented in India, just so much as the ten numerals, the very cornerstone of all present civilization, were discovered in India, and are in reality, Sanskrit words.

"In philosophy we are even now head and shoulders above any other nation, as Schopenhauer, the great German philosopher, has confessed. In music India gave to the world her system of notation, with the seven cardinal notes and the diatonic scale, all of which we enjoyed as early as 350 B.C., while it came to Europe only in the eleventh century. In philology, our Sanskrit language is now universally acknowledged to be the foundation of all European languages, which, in fact, are nothing but jargonized Sanskrit.

"In literature, our epics and poems and dramas rank as high as those of any language; our 'Shaguntala' [*Shakuntala*] was summarized by Germany's greatest poet, as 'heaven and earth united'. India has given to the world the fables of Aesop, which were copied by Aesop from an old Sanskrit book; it has given the Arabian Nights, yes, even the story of Cinderella and the Bean Stalks. In manufacture, India was the first to make cotton and purple [dye], it was proficient in all works of jewelry, and the very word 'sugar', as well as the article itself, is the product of India. Lastly she has invented the game of chess and the cards and the dice. So great, in fact, was the superiority of India in every respect, that it drew to her borders the hungry cohorts of Europe, and thereby indirectly brought about the discovery of America.

"And now, what has the world given to India in return for all that? Nothing but nullification [vilification] and curse and contempt. The world waded in her children's life-blood, it reduced India to poverty and her sons and daughters to slavery, and now it adds insult to injury by preaching to her a religion which can only thrive on the destruction of every other religion. But India is not afraid. It does not beg for mercy at the hands of any nation. Our only fault is that we cannot: fight to conquer; but we trust in the eternity of truth. India's message to the world is first of all, her blessing; she is returning good for the evil which is done her, and thus she puts into execution this noble idea, which had its origin in India. Lastly, India's message is, that calm goodness, patience and gentleness will ultimately triumph. For where are the Greeks, the onetime masters of the earth? They are gone. Where are the Romans, at the tramp of whose cohorts the world trembled? Passed away. Where are the Arabs, who in fifty years had carried their banners from the Atlantic to the Pacific? and where are the Spaniards, the cruel murderers of millions of men? Both races are nearly extinct; but thanks to the morality of her children, the kinder race will never perish, and she will yet see the hour of her triumph."

At the close of the lecture, which was warmly applauded, Swami Vivekananda answered a number of questions in regard to the customs of India. He denied positively the truth of the statement published in yesterday's [February 25] *Standard Union,* to the effect that widows are ill-treated in India. The law guarantees her not only her own property, before marriage, but also all she received from her husband, at whose death, if there be no direct heirs, the property goes to her. Widows seldom marry in India, because of the scarcity of men. He also stated that the self-sacrifices of wives at the death of their husbands as well as the fanatical self-destruction under the wheels of the Juggernaut, have wholly stopped, and referred his hearers for proof to Sir William Hunter's "History of the Indian Empire".

Child Widows Of India

(*Daily Eagle*, February 27, 1895)

Swami Vivekananda, the Hindu monk, lectured in Historical hall Monday night under the auspices of the Brooklyn Ethical association, on "India's Gift to the World". There were about two hundred and fifty people in the hall when the Swami stepped on the platform. Much interest was manifested on account of the denial by Mrs. James McKeen, president of the Brooklyn Ramabai circle, which is interested in Christian work in India, of the statement attributed to the lecture that the child widows of India were not protected [ill-treated]. In no part of his lecture was reference made to this denial, but after he had concluded, one of the audience asked the lecturer what explanation he had to make to the statement. Swami Vivekananda said that it was untrue that child widows were abused or ill treated in any way. He added:

"It is a fact that some Hindus marry very young. Others marry when they have attained a fair age and some do not marry at all. My grandfather was married when quite a child. My father when he was 14 years old and I am 30 years old and am not yet married. When a husband dies all his possessions go to his widow. If a widow is poor she is the same as poor widows in any other country. Old men sometimes marry children, but if the husband was wealthy it was all the better for the widow the sooner he died. I have traveled all over India, but failed to see a case of the ill treatment mentioned. At one time there were religious fanatics, widows, who threw themselves into a fire and were consumed by the flames at the death of their husbands. The Hindus did not believe in this, but did not prevent it, and it was not until the British obtained control of India that it was finally prohibited. These women were considered saints and in many instances monuments were erected to their memory."

Some Customs Of The Hindus

(Brooklyn Standard Union, April 8, 1895)

A special meeting of the Brooklyn Ethical Association with an address by Swami Vivekananda, the Hindu monk as the main feature, was held at the Pouch Gallery, of Clinton avenue, last night. "Some customs of the Hindus what they mean, and how they are misinterpreted," was the subject treated. A large throng of people filled the spacious gallery.

Dressed in his Oriental costume, his eyes bright, and a flush mantling his face, Swami Vivekananda started to tell of his people, of his country, and its customs. He desired only that justice be shown to him and to his. In the beginning of his discourse he said he would give a general idea of India. He said it was not a country but a continent; that erroneous ideas had been promulgated by travellers who had never seen the country. He said that there were nine separate languages spoken and over 100 different dialects. He spoke severely of those who wrote about his country, and said their brains were addled by superstition, and that they had an idea that everyone outside of the pale of their own religion was a horrible blackguard. One of the customs that had often been misinterpreted was the brushing of the teeth by the Hindus. They never put hair or skin in their mouths, but use a plant. "Hence a man wrote," said the speaker, "that the Hindus get up early in the morning and swallow a plant." He said the [custom of widows throwing themselves under the] car of juggernaut did not exist, never had, and that no one knew how such a story started.

Swami Vivekananda's talk on caste was most comprehensive and interesting. He said it was not a granted [graded] system of classes, but that each caste thought itself to be superior to all the others. He said it was a trade guild and not a religious institution. He said that it had been in existence from time immemorial, and explained how at first only certain rights were hereditary, but how afterward the ties were bound closer, and intermarriage and eating and drinking were restricted to each caste.

The speaker told of the effect that the mere presence of a Christian or Mohammedan would have on a Hindu household. He said that it was veritable pollution for a white man to step into a Hindu's presence, and that after receiving one outside of his religion, the Hindu always took a bath.

The Hindu monk abused [?] the order of the Pariahs roundly, saying they did all the menial work, ate carrion and were the scavengers. He also said that the people who wrote books on India came only into contact with these people, and not with genuine Hindus. He described the trial of one who broke the rules of caste, and said that the only punishment inflicted was the refusal of the particular caste to intermarry or drink or eat with him or his children. All other ideas were erroneous.

In explaining the defects of caste, the speaker said that in preventing competition it produced stagnation, and completely blocked the progress of the people. He said that in taking away brutality it stopped social improvements. In checking competition it increased population. In its favor, he said, were the facts that it was the only ideal of equality and fraternity. That money had nothing to do with social standing in the caste. All were equal. He said that the fault of all the great reformers was that they thought caste was due only to religious representation, instead of ascribing it to the right source, namely, the curious social conditions. He spoke very bitterly of the attempts of the English and Mohammedans to civilize the country by the bayonet and fire and sword. He said that to abolish caste one must change the social conditions completely ant destroy the entire economic system of the country. Better, he said, that the waves of the [Bay of] Bengal flow and drown all rather than this. English civilization was composed of the three "B's" — Bible, bayonet, and brandy. "That is civilization, and it has been carried to such an extent that the average income of a Hindu is 50 cents a month. Russia is outside, saying. 'Let's civilize a little,' and England goes on and on."

The monk grew excited as he walked up and down, talking rapidly about the way the Hindus had been treated. He scored the foreign educated Hindus, and described their return to their native land, "full of champagne and new ideas". He said that child-marriage was bad, because the West said so, and that the mother-in-law could torture her daughter-in-law with impunity, as the son could not interfere. He said that the foreigners took every opportunity to abuse the heathen, because they had so many evils of their own that they wanted to cover them up. He said that each nation must work out its own salvation, and that no one else could solve its problems.

In speaking of India's benefactors he asked whether America had ever heard of David Herr [Hare], who established the first college for women, and who had devoted so much of his life to education.

The speaker gave a number of Indian proverbs that were not at all complimentary to the English. In closing he made an earnest appeal for his land. He said:

"It matters not as long as India is true to herself and to her religion. But a blow has been struck at her heart by this awful godless West when she sends hypocrisy and atheism into her midst. Instead of sending bushels of abuses, carloads of vituperation and shiploads of condemnations, let an endless stream of love go forth. Let us all be men"